praise for
focus on the family marriage series

This marriage study series is pure Focus on the Family—
reliable, biblically sound and dedicated to reestablishing family values
in today's society. This series will no doubt help a multitude of couples
strengthen their relationship, not only with each other,
but also with God, the *creator* of marriage itself.

Bruce Wilkinson

Author, The BreakThrough Series: *The Prayer of Jabez,*
Secrets of the Vine and *A Life God Rewards*

In this era of such need, Dr. Dobson's team has produced solid,
helpful materials about Christian marriage. Even if they have been
through marriage studies before, every couple—married or engaged—
will benefit from this foundational study of life together. Thanks to
Focus on the Family for helping set us straight in this top priority.

Charles W. Colson

Chairman, Prison Fellowship Ministries

In my 31 years as a pastor, I've officiated at hundreds of weddings.
Unfortunately, many of those unions failed. I only wish the *Focus on the*
Family Marriage Series had been available to me during those years.
What a marvelous tool you as pastors and Christian leaders have
at your disposal. I encourage you to use it to assist those you
serve in building successful, healthy marriages.

H. B. London, Jr.

Vice President, Ministry Outreach/Pastoral Ministries
Focus on the Family

Looking for a prescription for a better marriage?
You'll enjoy this timely and practical series!

Dr. Kevin Leman

Author, *Sheet Music: Uncovering the Secrets of
Sexual Intimacy in Marriage*

The *Focus on the Family Marriage Series* is successful because it shifts
the focus from how to fix or strengthen a marriage to *who* can do it.
Through this study you will learn that a blessed marriage will be the
happy by-product of a closer relationship with the *creator* of marriage.

Lisa Whelchel

Author, *Creative Correction* and
The Facts of Life and Other Lessons My Father Taught Me

In a day and age where the covenant of marriage is so quickly tossed
aside in the name of incompatibility and irreconcilable differences, a
marriage Bible study that is both inspirational and practical is desperately
needed. The *Focus on the Family Marriage Series* is what couples are seeking.
I give my highest recommendation to this Bible study series that has the
potential to dramatically impact and improve marriages today. Marriage
is not so much about finding the right partner as it is about being the
right partner. These studies give wonderful biblical teachings for
helping those who want to learn the beautiful art of being and
becoming all that God intends in their marriage.

Lysa TerKeurst

President, Proverbs 31 Ministries
Author, *Capture His Heart* and *Capture Her Heart*

focus on the family® marriage series

the
model
marriage

Gospel Light

PUBLISHING STAFF
William T. Greig, Chairman
Kyle Duncan, Publisher
Dr. Elmer L. Towns, Senior Consulting Publisher
Pam Weston, Senior Editor
Patti Pennington Virtue, Associate Editor
Kathryn T. Schuh, Editorial Assistant
Hilary Young, Editorial Assistant
Bayard Taylor, M.Div., Senior Editor, Biblical and Theological Issues
Samantha A. Hsu, Cover and Internal Designer
Amy Simpson, Contributing Writer

table of contents

Foreword by Gary T. Smalley 6

Introduction 8

**Session One: Heroes Make the Right Choices—
Philippians 2:9-11** 11
> The right choices aren't always the easy choices, but they are
> the ones that a fulfilling marriage is built upon.

Session Two: The Mystery of Submission—Philippians 2:6-8 21
> Submission in marriage means willingly and lovingly serving
> your spouse even when it is difficult.

Session Three: The Mission of Self-Sacrifice—Romans 5:19 35
> True love involves sacrificing selfish desires for the good of
> your marriage.

Session Four: Christ Is Our Model—Ephesians 5:1-2 45
> Joy in your marriage is found through loving your spouse
> the way Christ loves His bride, the Church.

Leader's Discussion Guide 55

foreword

The most urgent mission field on Earth is not across the sea or even across the street—it's right where you live: in your home and family. Jesus' last instruction was to "make disciples of all nations" (Matthew 28:19). At the thought of this command, our eyes look across the world for our work field. That's not bad; it's just not *all*. God intended the home to be the first place of Christian discipleship and growth (see Deuteronomy 6:4-8). Our family members must be the *first* ones we reach out to in word and example with the gospel of the Lord Jesus Christ, and the fundamental way in which this occurs is through the marriage relationship.

Divorce, blended families, the breakdown of communication and the complexities of daily life are taking a devastating toll on the God-ordained institutions of marriage and family. We do not need to look hard or search far for evidence that even Christian marriages and families are also in a desperate state. In response to the need to build strong Christ-centered marriages and families, this series was developed.

Focus on the Family is well known and respected worldwide for its stead-fast dedication to preserving the sanctity of marriage and family life. I can think of no better partnership than the one formed by Focus on the Family and Gospel Light to produce the *Focus on the Family Marriage Series*. This series is well-written, biblically sound and right on target for guiding couples to explore the foundation God has laid for marriage and to see Him as the role model for the perfect spouse. Through these studies, seeds will be planted that will germinate in your heart and mind for many years to come.

In our practical, bottom-line culture, we often want to jump over the *why* and get straight to the *what*. We think that by *doing* the six steps or *learning* the five ways, we will reach the goal. But deep-rooted growth is slower and more purposeful and begins with a well-grounded understanding of God's divine design. Knowing why marriage exists is crucial to making the how-tos more effective. Marriage is a gift from God, a unique and distinct covenant relationship through which His glory and goodness can resonate, and it is only through knowing the architect and His plan that we will build our marriage on the surest foundation.

God created marriage; He has a specific purpose for it, and He is committed to filling with fresh life and renewed strength each union yielded to Him. God wants to gather the hearts of every couple together, unite them in love and walk them to the finish line—all in His great grace and goodness.

May God, in His grace, lead you into His truth, strengthening your lives and your marriage.

Gary T. Smalley
Founder and Chairman of the Board
Smalley Relationship Center

introduction

At the beginning of creation God "made them male and female." "For this reason a man will leave his father and mother and be united to his wife, and the two will become one flesh." So they are no longer two, but one.
Mark 10:6-8

The Model Marriage can be used in a variety of situations, including small-group Bible studies, Sunday School classes or counseling or mentoring situations. An individual couple can also use this book as an at-home marriage-building study.

Each of the four sessions contains four main components.

Session Overview

Tilling the Ground
This is an introduction to the topic being discussed—commentary and questions to direct your thoughts toward the main idea of the session.

Planting the Seed
This is the Bible study portion in which you will read Scripture and answer questions to help discover lasting truths from God's Word.

Watering the Hope
This is a time for discussion and prayer. Whether you are using the study at home as a couple, in a small group or in a classroom setting, talking about the lesson with your spouse is a great way to solidify the truth and plant it deeply into your hearts.

Harvesting the Fruit
As a point of action, this portion of the session offers suggestions on putting the truth of the Word into action in your marriage relationship.

Suggestions for Individual Couple Study

There are at least three options for using this study as a couple.

- It may be used as a devotional study that each spouse would study individually through the week; then on a specified day, come together and discuss what you have learned and how to apply it to your marriage.
- You might choose to study one session together in an evening and then work on the application activities during the rest of the week.
- Because of the short length of this study, it is a great resource for a weekend retreat. Take a trip away for the weekend, and study each session together, interspersed with your favorite leisure activities.

Suggestions for Group Study

There are many ways that this study can be used in a group situation. The most common way is in a small-group Bible study format. However, it can also be used in adult Sunday School class. However you choose to use it, there are some general guidelines to follow for group study.

- Keep the group small—five to six couples is probably the maximum.
- Ask couples to commit to regular attendance for the four weeks of the study. Regular attendance is a key to building relationships and trust in a group.
- Encourage participants *not* to share anything of a personal or potentially embarrassing nature without first asking the spouse's permission.
- Whatever is discussed in the group meetings is to be held in strictest confidence among group members only.

There are additional leader helps in the back of this book and in *The Focus on the Family Marriage Ministry Guide.*

Suggestions for Mentoring or Counseling Relationships

This study also lends itself for use in relationships where one couple mentors or counsels another couple.

- A mentoring relationship, where a couple that has been married for several years is assigned to meet on a regular basis with a younger couple, could be arranged through a system set up by a church or ministry.
- A less formal way to start a mentoring relationship is for a younger couple to take the initiative and approach a couple that exemplify a mature, godly marriage and ask them to meet with them on a regular basis. Or the reverse might be a mature couple that approaches a younger couple to begin a mentoring relationship.
- When asked to mentor, some might shy away and think that they could never do that, knowing that their own marriage is less than perfect. But just as we are to disciple new believers, we must learn to disciple married couples to strengthen marriages in this difficult world. The Lord has promised to be "with you always" (Matthew 28:20).
- Before you begin to mentor a couple, first complete the study yourselves. This will serve to strengthen your own marriage and prepare you for leading another couple.
- Be prepared to learn as much or more than the couple(s) you will mentor.

There are additional helps for mentoring relationships in *The Focus on the Family Marriage Ministry Guide.*

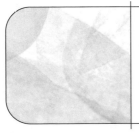

The Focus on the Family Marriage Series *is based on Al Janssen's* The Marriage Masterpiece *(Wheaton, IL: Tyndale House Publishers, 2001), an insightful look at what marriage can—and should—be. In this study, we are pleased to lead you through the wonderful journey of discovering the joy in your marriage that God wants you to experience!*

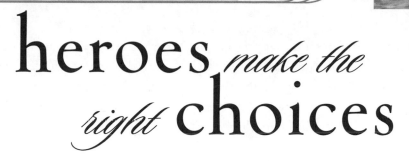

heroes *make the* *right* choices

Therefore God exalted him to the highest place and gave him the name
that is above every name, that at the name of Jesus every knee should bow,
in heaven and earth and under the earth, and every tongue confess that
Jesus Christ is Lord, to the glory of God the Father.
Philippians 2:9-11

When we think of heroes, we tend to think of those who make larger-than-life sacrifices for the good of others. They rush in to save the oppressed or the endangered with no thought to their own lives or safety.

In his book *The Marriage Masterpiece*, Al Janssen explained that a woman longs to "see her man ride in and save the day" and that "men long for a strong woman who will make them look good, not weak."[1] Every marriage needs a hero—a spouse who is willing to sacrifice his or her own temporal happiness for the good of the relationship.

tilling the ground

Children love to pretend that they are the superheroes they see on TV, rescuing others from near destruction. While boys may dream of saving the world from a dastardly enemy, girls often dream of a knight in shining armor who will ride in on a white horse and rescue them from danger; then they'll fall in love, get married and live happily ever after.

1. Who was your childhood hero—real or fictional?

   Why was this person a hero to you?

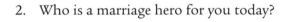

2. Who is a marriage hero for you today?

   What makes this person a hero?

3. How would you define a hero?

In our culture we equate getting married with living happily ever after. Unfortunately, too many couples head off to divorce court instead of becoming heroes and fighting for their marriage. According to an analysis by the National Survey of Families and Households, "86 percent of unhappily married people who stick it out find that, five years later, their marriages are happier."[2]

What Is a Godly Hero?

Each of us has daily opportunities to choose to do right or to do wrong; therefore, in the context of marriage, God calls every married couple to seek righteousness, or dying to self, instead of sin or self-centeredness. A godly hero is someone who ultimately seeks to do the will of God in all that he or she says and does: "For in him we live and move and have our being" (Acts 17:28).

4. What did God tell Adam in Genesis 2:16-17?

5. What occurred after God gave Adam this command, as described in the remainder of Genesis 2?

According to these verses in Genesis, Eve was created after Adam was given the command to "not eat from the tree of the knowledge of good and evil" (v. 17).

6. As you read Genesis 3:1-3, note the similarities and differences between what Eve told the serpent and what God told Adam in 2:16-17.

Do you think Adam passed along to Eve God's command regarding the tree of the knowledge of good and evil? Explain your answer.

7. According to Genesis 3:6, where was Adam when Eve ate the forbidden fruit?

How could Adam have been the hero in this situation?

Adam showed passiveness and even cowardice in the Garden of Eden when he failed to confront Eve and stop her from making the wrong choice. He compounded his lack of action when he *joined* her in disobeying God. God entrusted to Adam the care of the world and also to share with his wife the knowledge that God had given him, including this one command. When the moment of truth arrived, Adam acted as if he had never heard of the command.

8. Why is it difficult for one spouse to hold the other spouse accountable for his or her poor choices?

We each must make personal choices that will affect our relationship with God, but often when we make the wrong choices, the results have a detrimental effect on our human relationships and especially on our marriage.

Where then can we turn to find a model of a godly hero? To the Bible, of course!

9. Name at least three biblical heroes and explain why they are heroes.

10. What are some common characteristics of these heroes?

Our ultimate biblical hero is Jesus Christ. He gave up everything for His Bride.

11. How were Jesus' actions in Matthew 26:36-46 heroic in comparison to Adam and Eve's actions in Genesis 3:1-13?

The agony of Jesus described in Matthew 26 demonstrates the depths of His love for His Bride, the Church. He, who was sinless, died in our place for our sins so that we might live with Him for eternity.

How Can You Be a Hero?

Jesus is our role model as the heroic spouse.

12. How does Philippians 2:3-5 apply to marriage relationships?

13. According to Philippians 2:6-8, what did Christ give up for us?

14. What are some practical ways that humility and a Christlike attitude might be shown in a marriage?

Key points to remember when you are faced with the decision of whether or not to be a hero include

- **Courage**—Will you do the right thing and take whatever action is necessary for the long-term good of your marriage?
- **Strength**—Will you resist temptation and strive for righteousness?
- **Nobility**—Will you maintain honor and moral character, even if your spouse does not?

Consider the meaning of these key points and how they relate to your own attitudes and choices in your marriage.

"I can do everything through him who gives me strength" (Philippians 4:13). With this promise tucked deep within our hearts and minds, we can answer God's call to serve as heroes, making the right decisions—even when those decisions are difficult to make.

Heroism in a relationship is shown by daily making choices in the best interest of your spouse, building a respect that shows your spouse he or she can count on your commitment to your marriage. Heroism is also shown in sticking with someone through unusually rough times, as in the case of Dave and Sue.

Dave and Sue had the kind of marriage other couples aspired to. They were actively involved in church, devoted to their kids and appeared to enjoy each other's company. What looked like the perfect marriage on the surface was, in truth, on the brink of destruction.

After the birth of their third child, Sue became difficult to live with. One moment she was serene and happy and the next she was screaming and throwing things. Dave would often come home from work to find the children crying, the house a mess and no dinner preparations being made.

Dave's frustration at the situation became anger, resulting in increasing arguments with Sue. His vision for a happy marriage was drowned out by momentary feelings of apathy. He often thought, *What's the point? I've tried my hardest and paid my dues. Maybe I should just take the kids and leave Sue before we all self-destruct.* But he realized that he did love Sue and that there was something terribly wrong with her. He tried to get her to go to counseling or to see a doctor, but she just became more upset, withdrawing to their bedroom whenever he mentioned it. He also tried to do as much as possible around the house to ease her burden, but she seemed to resent that he was doing what she should be doing.

Finally, after a particularly difficult weekend, Dave opened up about his problems to his best friend, Ryan, who advised him to seek counseling for himself, even if Sue wouldn't go with him. It was during these counseling sessions that Dave learned that Sue was probably suffering from severe postpartum depression. After much prayer and loving encouragement, Sue agreed to a thorough physical exam which revealed that she had a chemical imbalance that was causing her depression. After a few months of antidepressant therapy and counseling, Sue was back to normal and their marriage relationship was once again thriving.[3]

15. How did Dave demonstrate a Christlike attitude?

16. What might have happened if Dave hadn't taken the initiative to seek counseling?

17. What are some other examples of how one spouse might make heroic choices for the sake of his or her spouse?

Every athlete knows that he or she can't be the hero unless he or she is actually playing in the game. In order to be the hero in your marriage, you must remain in the game, reminding yourself that it takes hard work, practice—yes, each decision serves as a practice for the next!—and sacrifice to win. We also have God's strength and wisdom to uphold us at every turn.

18. What are some reasons you might continue to play on a team during a game that your team is losing?

How could these reasons for staying in the game be applied to a marriage in which things are not going well?

Larger-than-life sacrifices will not likely be a part of your daily routine, but every decision you make that promotes the good of your spouse makes you a hero in your marriage. It's this kind of heroism that helps build and maintain a lasting marital relationship that honors God's plan for marriage.

harvesting the fruit

Should I really tell him I don't care about his stupid car or the details about how he "took it from a pile of junk and made a masterpiece"?

She's crying again! If she doesn't knock it off, I'm outta here!

Thoughts such as these will inevitably creep into our heads as we deal with the realities of living in close relationship with another person. When they do, we are faced with a choice between verbalizing our thoughts aloud or submitting them to God, asking His help to show compassionate love toward our spouse and to put his or her needs above our own (see Philippians 2:3-5).

In order to begin the process of stopping negative thoughts before damage can occur, decide for one day to mentally track the negative thoughts you have; and whenever one comes to mind, take decisive action to turn that thought over to God, asking Him to help "take captive every thought to make it obedient to Christ" (2 Corinthians 10:5). Memorizing this verse and other verses can help you replace negative thoughts with Christlike thoughts.

19. How has your spouse been a heroic model in your marriage?

20. How can you demonstrate the qualities of a hero—humility, compassion, courage, strength, nobility, Christlike attitudes, etc.—in your marriage?

Write down at least one practical action you will take during the next week to be a marriage hero to your spouse. Ask a friend to keep you accountable to this action.

Are there some actions or attitudes that you have shown toward your spouse for which you need to ask forgiveness? On a separate sheet of paper, write a letter asking for forgiveness from your spouse in specific areas that you know you have hurt him or her. After you and your spouse have shared your letters, pray together, asking for Christ's healing of your relationship and for His strength to make the right decisions in your marriage.

Notes
1. Al Janssen, *The Marriage Masterpiece* (Wheaton, IL: Tyndale House Publishers, 2001), p. 44.
2. Linda J. Waite and Maggie Gallagher, *The Case for Marriage* (New York: Doubleday, 2000), p. 148.
3. This is a compilation of several stories. Any resemblance to an actual situation is purely coincidental.

the mystery of
submission

Who, being in very nature God, did not consider equality with God something
to be grasped, but made himself nothing, taking the very nature of a servant,
being made in human likeness. And being found in appearance as a man,
he humbled himself and became obedient to death—even death on a cross!

Philippians 2:6-8

What comes to mind when you think of the word "submission"? Perhaps you shudder and the picture of a doormat immediately comes to mind. However, "doormat" and "submission" have distinctly different meanings. A person who acts as a doormat is "one that submits without protest to abuse and indignities."[1] A person who acts in submission yields "oneself to the authority or will of another."[2] A doormat chooses to allow him- or herself to be walked on, while submission is an act of the will to yield to the authority of another person.

"Submission" does not mean that one must endure a disrespectful or unloving relationship (as a doormat would). Instead, the term "submission" is used in the Bible to describe an aspect of our relationship with other believers—we are told to "submit to one another out of reverence for Christ" (Ephesians 5:21). It also describes one of the major aspects of our relationship with God (see James 4:7) and an aspect of heavenly wisdom (see James 3:17). We are also instructed to be submissive to those in authority over us (see Romans 13:1-5). Jesus Christ asks us to reflect His heart by willingly serving others, even if they don't deserve it—and this should especially apply to the way a husband and wife are to treat one another.

tilling the ground

Submitting to another person is probably one of the hardest things for us humans to learn to do. It is especially hard if the person to whom we must submit is a tyrant!

1. Have you ever had to be under submission to a difficult boss or teacher? Describe the experience (without naming names!) and explain what it taught you.

2. Have you ever had to train someone to submit to your authority? Was it an easy task? Why or why not?

    What did you learn from the experience?

3. Why do you think submission to another's authority is difficult?

God has set down standards of submission in all relationships. He has also provided us a model of submission through Christ, who said, "For I have come down from heaven not to do my will but to do the will of him who sent me" (John 6:38).

How many times have you heard someone say, "It's not fair!" and then some-one else retort, "Who says life's supposed to be fair"? Probably too many to count! But when you think about it, if life were truly fair, *none* of us would ever get to heaven!

Jesus relinquished His power and knowledge in heaven to come into this world in human form (see Philippians 2:6-8 and Hebrews 2:9-11). In doing so, He submitted to the will of God the Father.

The book of Ephesians has much to teach us about how to live out the Christian life, and it gives very specific instructions to husbands and wives.

4. According to Ephesians 5:21, to whom are we to submit?

How can submission to others show reverence for Christ?

Mutual submission in a marriage not only preserves order and harmony in the relationship but also increases love and respect between a husband and wife. Whether you are the husband or the wife, knowing your marital duties and responsibilities is essential for a healthy marriage. When both the husband and wife submit to their roles as defined by God, each ends up serv-ing the other and both find true contentment.

The Submissive Life

"Wives, submit to your husbands as to the Lord. For the husband is the head of the wife as Christ is the head of the church, his body, of which he is the Savior. Now as the church submits to Christ, so also wives should submit to their husbands in everything" (Ephesians 5:22-24).

Submission

Perhaps no other teaching in the Bible has caused more rancor between the sexes than these verses. The women's liberation movement screams in protest at the thought of submission to a husband. But let's examine the concept of submission.

5. What do you think submission means in the context of these verses in Ephesians?

6. How can a wife be submissive without allowing her husband to use her as a doormat?

7. How does a wife's allowing her husband to be the leader in the marriage serve to strengthen the marriage?

8. What must be given up in order to empower someone else?

9. What is the husband's responsibility that would make submission easier for the wife?

10. What might be a benefit of a wife's submission to her husband as described in 1 Peter 3:1-2?

Submission is a response that empowers the husband to be the leader that God has commanded him to be. When done in the context of Christ's obedience to God, submission will not be difficult—and remember, God will give you the strength to accomplish His will in your life (see Philippians 4:13).

Respect

"The wife must respect the husband" (Ephesians 5:33).

11. How does showing respect differ from being submissive?

12. Why do you suppose Paul added this admonition to wives?

A woman in biblical submission is acting out of respect for her husband and the role he has assumed under God's direction.

Help

The Lord God said, "It is not good for the man to be alone. I will make a helper suitable for him" (Genesis 2:18). When God created Eve, He did not create her as a slave to Adam. Nor did He create her from "the dust of the ground" (Genesis 2:7) as He did Adam. Instead, God took a part of Adam and formed Eve from it (see vv. 21-22). Eve was literally "bone of my bones and flesh of my flesh" to Adam (Genesis 2:23)—an equal to him, given to him by God so that he would have a partner on Earth.

13. What comes to mind when you think of the word "helper"?

Why do you suppose God used the word "helper" to describe Eve's role?

14. In what ways is a wife a partner to her husband?

15. According to Titus 2:4-5, what five responsibilities did Paul encourage older women to teach younger women in regard to their marriage and family?

Why are these attributes important in building a marriage and raising a family?

The wife is instructed to be submissive, show respect and be a helper to the husband. Now let's examine the husband's role.

The Spiritual Leader

"Wives, submit to your husbands as to the Lord. For the husband is the head of the wife as Christ is the head of the church" (Ephesians 5:22-23). This may sound like a carte-blanche ticket for men to lord it over their wives, but with this role comes a tremendous amount of responsibility. A husband must protect, care for and even give his life for his wife, just as Jesus did. So what do these instructions mean to husbands?

Sacrifice

"Husbands, love your wives, just as Christ loved the church and gave himself up for her" (Ephesians 5:25). Like Jesus, the husband must lay down his life for his bride. In practical terms, this means setting aside his selfish desires to fulfill the desires of his wife.

Another way a husband can show sacrifice is to adopt an attitude of humility, accepting that his weaknesses will be complemented by his wife's strengths. For example, the husband might be great at fixing things, but he can't manage the family budget; the wife, however, can stretch a dollar further than anyone. Thus, the husband would be wise to humbly turn the responsibility of the family finances over to his wife. For some men that might be a fearful thing because they might think they are losing control of their life.

16. Read Ephesians 5:28. What does it mean for a husband to love his wife as he loves himself?

Why is it difficult to love someone else if you do not love yourself?

17. What is one area in which your spouse is stronger than you in his or her abilities? How could you affirm your spouse in his or her areas of strength?

Protection

"After all, no one ever hated his own body, but he feeds and cares for it, just as Christ does the church" (Ephesians 5:29). Husbands are told to love and care for their wives to the degree that Christ loved the Church. *That's* a tall order; however, it is easier done when the husband has an intimate relationship with God and His Word.

18. What are some things that can build a hedge of protection around your marriage?

19. Read Ephesians 6:10-18. In what ways could a husband apply each piece of the armor of God to protect his wife and family?

Belt of truth

Breastplate of righteousness

Shoes of the gospel of peace

Shield of faith

Helmet of salvation

Sword of the Spirit

God knows all of the potential pitfalls and dangers in life that can snag your daily steps, so He urges husbands to feed and care for their wives by building a hedge of protection between the world's disarray and their Christ-centered marriage. This hedge of protection can include conflict-resolution skills, financial planning and Bible studies (like this one!)—anything that strengthens your bond with your spouse and with God is another branch in your hedge of protection.

Holiness

The husband is also admonished "to make [his wife] holy, cleansing her by the washing with water through the word, and to present her to himself as a radiant church, without stain or wrinkle or any other blemish, but holy and blameless" (Ephesians 5:26-27). This is probably the most important—and most difficult—role for a husband to perform. He is ordained to be the spiritual leader of the family.

20. Even the most important relationship in your life should not be more important than your relationship with God. Who or what comes first in your life?

21. How can a husband follow the instructions in Ephesians 5:25-33?

God designed marriage to be an equal partnership in which each spouse takes on a different set of responsibilities. While the husband is called to put aside his own interests to care for his wife, the wife is called to willingly follow her husband's lead. When each spouse willingly assumes his or her God-given role in the marriage, each will be uplifted and gratified in the relationship— as God designed.

watering the hope

We are not asked to do anything for our spouse that Jesus has not already done for His Bride, the Church. Just as a wife is instructed to submit to her husband, Jesus humbled Himself to the will of God the Father. And a husband is to love sacrificially just as Jesus did by dying on the cross in order to give us hope and eternal life.

Rest assured that God will not leave you without the resources to do His will in regard to your duties as a husband or a wife—or, for that matter, as a believer living in obedience to God. "If any of you lacks wisdom, he should ask God, who gives generously to all without finding fault, and it will be given him" (James 1:5). He will also help you when you are tempted to sin (see 1 Corinthians 10:13).

22. How have you experienced God's providing you with what you needed in order to accomplish what He has instructed you to do?

What do you need from God right now to help you obey His commands in your marriage?

23. As a result of Jesus' submission to the will of God, Philippians 2:9 tells us "God exalted him to the highest place and gave him the name that is above every name." What might your rewards be when you continually show your love through submitting to God's will and serving your spouse?

24. Submission and servanthood are often viewed as characteristics of someone who is inferior to others. What are the characteristics of someone who submits to the will of God and serves others unselfishly?

Who is an example to you of someone who lives out the commands of Ephesians 5:21-33 in his or her life and marriage? How has this person impacted you and your marriage?

It is our attitude that determines how we relate to others in all aspects of our life. Are we kind or critical? Do we love or hate? Are we angry or content? Are we quick to judge or do we give the benefit of the doubt?

harvesting the fruit

Jesus gave these final instructions to His disciples: "If you love me, you will obey what I command. And I will ask the Father, and he will give you another Counselor to be with you forever—the Spirit of truth" (John 14:15-17). If you heed His Word in your marriage—love and obey God—you and your spouse will never be alone, fighting the world without the help of your heavenly Father. Why? Because you are submitting to Him, which allows the Lord to fulfill His plan in your relationship. You will live with the Holy Spirit in your life, and He will steer you toward a healthy and fulfilling marriage.

25. Write (on a separate piece of paper if you need to) an affirmation of your love and commitment to your spouse. Thank him or her for what he or she does to demonstrate God's love to you.

Plan a quiet romantic time to share with your spouse what you have written. Pray together, thanking God for how your spouse blesses you. Commit to one another that you will affirm (compliment) each other when you notice your spouse demonstrating Christlike behavior—and *do* it!

26. Husbands: Write down one way in which you can demonstrate sacrificial service to your wife this week.

    Wives: Write down one way in which you can demonstrate submission to your husband this week.

Share your plan with an accountability partner of the same gender. Be sure to call this person during the week to see how he or she is doing and to share how you are doing.

Notes

1. *Merriam-Webster's Collegiate Dictionary*, 10th edition, s.v. "doormat."
2. *Merriam-Webster's Collegiate Dictionary*, 10th edition, s.v. "submission."

the mission of self-sacrifice

For just as through the disobedience of the one man [Adam] the many were made sinners, so also through the obedience of the one man [Jesus] the many will be made righteous.

Romans 5:19

Who could forget the faces of the firefighters captured in photos as they trudged up the stairs of the World Trade Center towers—probably knowing full well that they were climbing to their own deaths on that terrifying day: September 11, 2001. And who could forget the recorded voices of the airline passengers who made the sacrificial decision to fight off the hijackers, assuring their own deaths as they crashed the plane in a Pennsylvania field, to avoid further loss of lives in Washington, D.C. There are thousands of similar stories of people who courageously and sacrificially gave up their lives for others in the face of certain death on 9/11.

On the other hand, we need look no further than our TV sets to find glimpses of the extremes of selfishness of society: reality, talent and game shows. In many of these shows, people are encouraged to turn against one another to survive, or they allow emcees to heap insults on them for the chance to become a millionaire or a star. And as if you need any further examples of extreme selfishness, just try to drive the speed limit on our nation's roads!

One of the cornerstones of a healthy marriage must be self-sacrifice, but our human nature strains against the call to sacrifice our personal needs and comfort for the good of our spouse—and our relationship.

Self-sacrifice is something that is so seldom experienced in daily life that when we hear of someone sacrificing him- or herself for the good of others, everyone seems genuinely surprised and even puzzled. Yet every day most parents work sacrificially to provide for their children, and police officers and firefighters put their lives on the line to protect us or to rescue people in dangerous situations—examples of self-sacrifice abound if we would look around us.

1. How would you define "sacrifice"?

    How would you define "*self*-sacrifice"?

2. Think about the people you observe on a regular basis. List some examples of self-sacrifice that you see in everyday life.

3. Who has sacrificed their own selfish desires to help you? Give specific examples of what they have done for you.

One person's sacrifice can make the difference for all involved—and one person's decision to act selfishly can lead to disaster, which is what ultimately happened when Adam and Eve chose to eat from the forbidden tree rather than sacrifice their own desires to taste the one fruit that God commanded them not to eat.

planting the seed

The Ultimate Sacrifice

There is no greater sacrifice than when one person gives his or her own life to save another. Jesus told His disciples, "Greater love has no one than this, that he lay down his life for his friends" (John 15:13).

Dying for someone else is something we'd all like to think we would do for those we love, but who would give up his or her own life for the sake of a complete stranger or, even more unlikely, an enemy! Yet that's exactly what Jesus did, not for only one person, but for everyone.

4.   Read and summarize Romans 3:22-23.

Salvation begins by understanding that we have sinned and fallen far short of God's perfect plan for our lives. We are lost in our own rebellion and cannot save ourselves no matter how hard we try.

5.   What does Romans 5:6-8 tell us about the purpose of Jesus' sacrificial death on the cross?

6. What does Romans 6:23 say about the result of sin, and what does God offer to us?

The good news is that God sent His only Son, Jesus Christ, to provide us with complete redemption from sin. Jesus' sinless life is a model for us; His death for our sins provide salvation for all who will believe: "For God so loved the world that he gave his one and only Son, that whoever believes in him shall not perish but have eternal life" (John 3:16).

7. What does Romans 10:9-13 say about how to express belief in Jesus?

Because salvation is a gift offered by our gracious God, our only response should be to graciously receive it.

8. Can you say with confidence that Jesus is your Lord?
   ☐ Yes   ☐ No

If you have already accepted Jesus as your Savior, describe when and how that happened.

If you have never accepted Jesus Christ as Savior, won't you consider receiving Him by faith right now? The Bible is clear that when we come to the Lord, He will receive us. Take a moment and consider the truths that have been discussed here and what you must do in response. Discuss any questions you might have with a pastor, Christian friend or the leader of this study.

Christ died for us, even when we were still sinners! There is no sacrifice that can begin to compare to the one made by Jesus Christ on the cross at Calvary. He gave His life so that we might live eternally—in heaven—with

Him. This selfless act by our Savior puts the kind of sacrifice that God expects from us in our marriage into a new perspective, doesn't it?

The Sacrifice of Self

We probably will never be asked to die physically for our spouse, but in a sense we should die to our selfish nature on a daily basis. When we accept Jesus as our Savior and make Him Lord of our life, we are identified with Him. "The death he died, he died to sin once for all; but the life he lives, he lives to God. In the same way, count yourselves dead to sin but alive to God in Christ Jesus" (Romans 6:10-11). When we selfishly want our own needs and desires satisfied to the detriment of our spouse and our marriage relationship, we are not dead to sin as we should be.

9. How does Ephesians 5:21 relate to dying to our selfish nature?

10. How can each of the following commands be practically applied to marriage? (You will have an opportunity to apply these to your own marriage in the end of this session.)

Romans 12:10

Romans 12:15

Romans 12:18

1 Corinthians 10:24

Philippians 2:3-4

Colossians 3:12-14

Colossians 3:17

11. How might Ephesians 4:29,31-32 apply to serving one's spouse?

12. How could Matthew 25:34-40 be applied to sacrificial love in a marriage?

A marriage is satisfying only to the degree that a husband and wife are willing to sacrifice, each for the other, on a daily basis. Whatever we do to others, we do to God—whether we are serving them in love or tearing them down.

13. Read Paul's prayer in Ephesians 3:14-21. How could this prayer be applied to sacrificially serving a spouse?

In *The Marriage Masterpiece*, Al Janssen states, "The selfish spouse insists on being served. The humble spouse becomes a servant."[1] It is only through the Holy Spirit's power in your life that you will be able to serve your spouse as Christ serves His Bride, the Church.

watering the hope

In each of the following situations, describe how a spouse might respond in love:

14. While Cathy was putting the final touches on the tasty meal that she had worked on all afternoon, she asked Charles to round up the children and make sure they washed their hands for dinner. He angrily snapped at her, "Why should I have to do that? The kids are your responsibility. I just got home, and I'm tired from working hard all day. All you have to do is keep the house and kids in order! You go round them up and let me read the paper in peace!"

15. As Tyler sat down and reached for the TV remote control, he was relishing the chance to see his favorite team finally get to play for the championship. He'd even worked overtime and rearranged his work schedule so that he could have tonight off. He was surprised to see nothing but snow on the TV screen. As he switched channels with no improvement, he called to his wife, "Lindy, what's wrong with the TV?" She answered, "Oh, I'm sorry, Honey. I forgot to pay the bill, so they cut the service!"

16. Miranda had been looking forward to their special night out all week. She and Bill didn't often have the money to go to dinner and a play. They had scrimped and saved to afford the tickets to the hottest play in the city. Miranda was concerned that it was getting late—if Bill

didn't come home soon, they might have to skip dinner at the restaurant. Finally, Bill trudged through the door, looking beat. "What happened?" Miranda demanded. "Why are you so late?" "My boss dropped a huge rush job on me at the last minute," Bill answered. "Now I can't go tonight because I have to finish it before tomorrow morning. Not only that, the car broke down about a mile from the house, and I had to walk the rest of the way home!" Miranda began to cry when she realized their special evening was ruined.

In every marriage there will be times when one spouse must extend grace to the other for disappointments or bad behavior. At times like this, it is advantageous to remember the grace God has extended to you—salvation through Jesus Christ's excruciating death on the cross!

 harvesting the fruit

In the deepest corners of our souls, we long to be the recipient of sacrificial love from someone who loves us so deeply that he or she is willing to risk it all—even life—for us. Ironically, all of us have already received this ultimate gift of love—from Jesus Christ.

Our relationship with our spouse needs to have that same selfless spirit that Jesus Christ has toward us—a willingness to die to our own selfish desires. We need to have the mind of Christ which counters our normal selfish tendencies to demand *our* rights.

17. Describe a time when you knew you had to humble yourself but felt like praying, "God, not today—please! Why can't today be about *me?*" What did you do?

18. Give specific actions that you might do to express the truth of the following Scripture passages:

Romans 12:10

Romans 12:15

Romans 12:18

1 Corinthians 10:24

Philippians 2:3-4

Colossians 3:12-14

Colossians 3:17

At times it can be hard to serve your spouse. This week, think about one instance in which you could serve your spouse sacrificially. Don't share the situation with your spouse; instead, take it to God in thoughtful prayer and ask His direction for how to resolve the issue in your heart.

Whenever a particular situation in which you find it difficult to sacrifice your desires for those of your spouse arises, ask the Lord to help you "make every effort to do what leads to peace and to mutual edification" (Romans 14:19).

19. List ways that your spouse has sacrificially served you.

Have you ever thanked your spouse for showing selfless love? Spend a few moments sharing your list with your spouse; then pray together, thanking God for the gift He has given you in each other. Also thank Him for the gift of eternal life that He has given you through Jesus' sacrificial death for your sins.

Note

1. Al Janssen, *The Marriage Masterpiece* (Wheaton, IL: Tyndale House Publishers, 2001), p. 150.

Christ *is our* model

Be imitators of God, therefore, as dearly loved children and live a life of love, just as
Christ loved us and gave himself up for us as a fragrant offering and sacrifice to God.
Ephesians 5:1-2

This key verse tells us that we are called to love just like Christ. Isn't it interesting that His sacrifice is described as "fragrant"? How could such a terrible,
cruel death be described "as a fragrant offering." Despite the horrific scenes
of His death, we can rejoice in His sacrifice because we know it was a gift with
the qualities of a sweet and delicate offering.

Does the fragrance of Christ emanate from your marriage? Although
Christ was never married, we can look to Him as the perfect model for how
to sacrificially love and submit to our spouse.

The marriage relationship is one of God's primary means of showing His divine nature to the world. Have you ever seen a devoted couple that lovingly worked together to show the love of God to others? The world takes notice when a man and a woman truly love each other the way Christ loves the Church.

1. Whose marriage has shown you the love of Christ?

2. What are the characteristics of a Christlike marriage?

3. How could your marriage reflect God's love for all people?

We have a choice in every difficult situation: We can succumb to the emotions of the moment, or we can turn our emotions, thoughts and actions over to God and experience His joy.

Because of the Fall, God's original intention for marriage has been clouded over and can't be completely grasped; however, we need only read His Word to discover His heart for marriage.

Committed

"I gave you my solemn oath and entered into a covenant with you" (Ezekiel 16:8). God didn't just reveal Himself to Israel; He entered into a binding covenant with her, a commitment so binding that God Himself agreed to pay the price—death to the one who broke the covenant—if the promise were broken. He fulfilled that promise by sending Jesus to Earth to die for our sins; and yet, we were the ones who deserved to die for breaking the covenant!

4.   Read Matthew 6:19-21. How does this verse apply to your relationship with God? What are your treasures—what is most important to you?

5.   Do you remember your marriage vows? What did you vow to your spouse at your wedding?

God is able to serve as our exemplary model for marriage because He has demonstrated it for us through His covenant marriage to Israel. This covenant commitment is the very foundation of marriage as God intended.

Devoted

"Has not the LORD made them one? In flesh and spirit they are his. And why one? Because he was seeking godly offspring. So guard yourself in your spirit, and do not break faith with the wife of your youth" (Malachi 2:15). God's purpose for marriage—the bond between man and woman, and their raising godly children—is foiled when we break faith with our marriage covenant. Just as God promises steadfast devotion to His people, we are to mirror the same unconditional devotion to our marriage partner.

6. How does Matthew 19:4-6 show God's plan for marriage?

   If a husband or wife even *considers* divorce as an option for resolving marital issues, how does this harm the relationship between the couple?

7. Psalm 85:10 is a lovely picture of God's desired relationship with His people. In what ways could the following four qualities be shown in actions that would enhance a marriage?

   Love

   Faithfulness

   Righteousness

   Peace

It is God's purpose for marriage that "love and faithfulness never leave you" (Proverbs 3:3). Ultimately, it is your attitude and actions that will reveal whether you are truly loving and faithful and if your spouse truly trusts and knows that your love is a lasting commitment.

Forgiving

"Bear with each other and forgive whatever grievances you may have against one another. Forgive as the Lord forgave you" (Colossians 3:13). God knows how difficult it is for you to forgive others—especially when a loved one has wronged you. However, He asks no more of you than He continually demonstrates in forgiving your sins against Him. We are called to forgive those who hurt us because we have been the recipients of His forgiveness over and over again.

8. According to Ephesians 4:32, why are we to be forgiving?

How much has God forgiven you in Christ Jesus?

9. Read Matthew 6:14, Mark 11:25 and Luke 6:37. Why did Jesus emphasize the importance of forgiveness in our relationships?

A forgiving spirit demonstrates that you have received God's love and forgiveness and that you recognize the sacrifice paid for your sins through Christ. When you think about it, the total amount of forgiveness you are asked to demonstrate in your lifetime will never equal one moment of Christ's agony on the cross for *you*.

10. Read Malachi 2:13-16. What potential pitfall does God sternly warn against in this passage?

11. Why do you think God hates divorce? (See Malachi 2:16; Matthew 19:8; 1 Corinthians 7:10-12).

Meaning

God never gave up on His marriage relationship with His people. In fact He paid the highest price; He sacrificed His Son, Jesus, to pay the price of the broken covenant. Why did Jesus die for us? He didn't do it for personal happiness; He suffered agony both before and during His crucifixion. He endured the suffering for our sakes and for future hope of happiness. "Let us fix our eyes on Jesus, the author and perfecter of our faith, who *for the joy* set before him endured the cross, scorning its shame, and sat down at the right hand of the throne of God" (Hebrews 12:2, emphasis added).

Personal happiness can be a by-product of marriage, but it is not the sole purpose of marriage. True meaning in marriage is not found by pursuing happiness or self-fulfillment; it is discovered by practicing self-sacrifice. "This is the challenge for marriage—to sacrifice my momentary definition of happiness for the long-term good of my spouse, thus reflecting God's heart and earning His praise, 'Well done, good and faithful servant.' "[1]

12. What is the difference between happiness and joy?

13. According to James 1:2-4, why are we supposed to be joyful in difficult times?

In James 1:12, what is the blessing to those who persevere under trial?

14. How can difficult times bring purpose and meaning to a marriage relationship?

God wants us to succeed in our marriage! With His help we can keep our marriage covenant and do so with great joy. God wants us to passionately stay in tune with our spouse, to discover whatever is holding us captive—whether it be a lack of commitment, devotion, forgiveness or meaning—and to set us free.

watering the hope

Consider the true story of David and Vi.

> David and Vi met at church in the 1930s, and their courtship occurred around church events. They were married at the start of World War II. In the 1960s, Vi began to have problems with forgetfulness and anxiety. In the early 70s she was diagnosed with

Alzheimer's. She began to slowly deteriorate, but David continued to care for her. Despite the urging of friends as she deteriorated more and more, he refused to have her put in a nursing home. He hired nursing care for the hours he was at work but then took over her care at night. David's love for Vi probably kept her alive for the nearly 15 years that she suffered from the disease. In the end, David died first of a brain tumor, but Vi joined him in heaven 43 hours later. His children noted that their father became a gentler man during his wife's illness.

The greatest legacy that David left to his children and his community was his example of sacrificial love for the final 15 years of his marriage to Vi. His actions showed the power of love and covenant. [2]

15. What about the story of David and Vi encourages you?

16. What was the fruit of David's devotion to his wife?

17. Do you know a couple like David and Vi? How could you be of help to such a couple?

Sacrificial love can be demonstrated in a variety of ways—from a subtle change of attitude to the daily care of a terminally ill spouse. Whatever form of expression, the sacrificial love you show to your spouse (and others) will bear fruit for God's kingdom.

"Guard yourself in your spirit, and do not break faith" (Malachi 2:15-16). This is how we can stay committed to following Christ's example. We must have the same commitment to marriage that God had for His people. Commitment is the door, and Christ is the key that will unlock the possibility for you to experience a truly fulfilled and committed marriage.

18. How does Colossians 3:1-2 relate to Jesus as your role model for loving sacrificially?

19. What steps will you take *today* to ensure that with the love of Jesus you unlock the door to a fulfilling marriage?

> *As water reflects a face, so a man's heart reflects the man.*
> Proverbs 27:19

The ultimate goal for your marriage should be that it reflects Christ's image. Make a date with your spouse to discuss one or two areas in which you do not see eye-to-eye on a particular issue. Plan for this time together, outlining issues to be discussed and making a pact with your spouse that this time will not serve as a time to argue over differing points of view;

instead, it will be a time to find understanding or a solution for the situation. If you find yourself becoming argumentative in your discussion, reign yourself in with Solomon's wisdom: "A man's pride will bring him low, but the humble in spirit will retain honor" (Proverbs 29:23, *NKJV*)!

Notes

1. Al Janssen, *The Marriage Masterpiece* (Wheaton, IL: Tyndale House Publishers, 2001), p. 156.

2. Ibid., pp. 129-131.

leader's discussion guide

General Guidelines

1. If at all possible, the group should be led by a married couple. This does not mean that both spouses need to be leading the discussions; perhaps one spouse is better at facilitating discussions while the other is better at relationship building or organization—but the leader couple should share responsibilities wherever possible.

2. At the first meeting, be sure to lay down the ground rules for discussions, stressing that following these rules will help everyone feel comfortable during discussion times.
   a. No one should share anything of a personal or potentially embarrassing nature without first asking his or her spouse's permission.
   b. Whatever is discussed in the group meetings is to be held in strictest confidence among group members only.
   c. Allow everyone in the group to participate. However, as a leader, don't force anyone to answer a question if he or she is reluctant. Be sensitive to the different personalities and communication styles among your group members.

3. Fellowship time is very important in building small-group relationships. Providing beverages and/or light refreshments either before or after each session will encourage a time of informal fellowship.

4. Most people live very busy lives; respect the time of your group members by beginning and ending meetings on time.

The Focus on the Family Marriage Ministry Guide *has even more information on starting and leading a small group. You will find this an invaluable resource as you lead others through this Bible study.*

How to Use the Material

1. Each session has more than enough material to cover in a 45-minute teaching period. You will probably not have time to discuss every single question in each session, so prepare for each meeting by selecting questions you feel are most important to address for your group; discuss other questions as time permits. Be sure to save the last 10 minutes of your meeting time for each couple to interact individually and to pray together before adjourning.

   Optional Eight-Session Plan—You can easily divide each session into two parts if you'd like to cover all of the material presented in each session. Each section of the session has enough questions to divide in half, and the Bible study sections (Planting the Seed) are divided into two or three sections that can be taught in separate sessions.

2. Each spouse should have his or her own copy of the book in order to personally answer the questions. The general plan of this study is that the couples complete the questions at home during the week and then bring their books to the meeting to share what they have learned during the week.

   However, the reality of leading small groups in this day and age is that some members will find it difficult to do the homework. If you find that to be the case with your group, consider adjusting the lessons and having members complete the study during your meeting time as you guide them through the lesson. If you use this method, be sure to encourage members to share their individual answers with their spouses during the week (perhaps on a date night).

A Note to Leaders: This Bible study series is based on The Marriage Masterpiece[1] *by Al Janssen. We highly recommend that you read chapters 14 and 15 in preparation for leading this study.*

Before the Meeting

1. Gather materials for making name tags. Also gather pens or pencils, paper, 3x5-inch index cards and Bibles.
2. Make photocopies of the Prayer Request Form (found in *The Focus on the Family Marriage Ministry Guide*, "Reproducible Forms" section) or provide index cards for recording requests.
3. Read through your own answers from the session and mark the ones that you especially want to have the group discuss. Also highlight any key verses you feel are appropriate to share.
4. Prepare slips of paper with references for the verses that you will want someone to read aloud during the session. Distribute these slips as group members arrive, but be sensitive to those who are uncomfortable reading aloud or who might not be familiar with the Bible.
5. Collect items needed for either of the ice-breaker games (see below).

Ice Breakers

1. If this is the first meeting for this couples group, have everyone introduce themselves and tell the group a brief summary of how they met their spouse, how long they have been married and one interesting fact about their spouse. Be sure to remind them not to reveal anything about their spouse that the spouse would be uncomfortable sharing him- or herself.
2. On separate slips of paper, write the names of fictional or real heroes or heroines (e.g., Superman, Mighty Mouse, Wonder Woman, police officer, rescue worker, etc.). You can play the game in one of two ways:

a. **Option 1:** Play a game of Pictionary. You will need a white board or large newsprint pad and the appropriate felt-tip pens. Have group members form two teams. The first person draws pictures to get his or her team members to guess the name of the hero. Allow only 30 seconds for members to draw.

b. **Option 2:** You will need masking tape to attach the slips of paper to the backs of members as they arrive. Allow them about five minutes to go around the room asking other group members yes-or-no questions to try to figure out the character's name that is attached to their back.

3. Begin in prayer.

Discussion

1. **Tilling the Ground**—This section is for getting the group involved in the topic at hand. The questions will usually be of a lighter tone. Discuss questions 1 through 3.

2. **Planting the Seed**—This section is the Bible study and is intended to give the biblical concepts for the session. For a little fun, ask for four volunteers to act out the Genesis 3 story as you read it aloud. The characters are Adam, Eve, the serpent and the tree. Be sure to read slowly enough for them to act out what you read. After the volunteers have been applauded for their great acting skills, discuss questions 4 through 14.

4. **Watering the Hope**—The case study and questions in this section will help members bring the Bible study into the reality of their own expectations versus God's plan. Don't neglect this part of the study, as it brings the whole lesson into the here and now, applying God's Word to daily life.

   Have the whole group discuss questions 15 through 18.

5. **Harvesting the Fruit**—This section is meant to help the individual couples apply the lesson to their own marriages and can be dealt with in several ways.

   a. Allow the couples one-on-one time at the end of the meeting. This would require space for them to be alone, with enough space between couples to allow for quiet, private conversations.

If couples have already answered the questions individually, now would be the time to share their answers. Give a time limit, emphasizing that their discussions can be continued at home if they are not able to answer all of the questions in the time allotted.

If couples have not answered the questions before the meeting, have them answer them together now. This works best when there is open-ended time for the couples to stay until they have completed their discussion and will require that the leaders stay until the last couple has finished.

b. Instruct couples to complete this section at home during the week after the meeting. This will give them quiet and private time to deal with any issues that might come up and to spend all the time needed to complete the discussion. You will want to follow up at the next meeting to hold couples accountable for completing this part of the lesson.

c. At times it might be advantageous to pair up two couples to discuss these questions. This would help build accountability into the study.

Allow time for the individual couples to meet together to complete this section of the questions.

6. **Close in Prayer**—An important part of any small-group relationship is the time spent in prayer for one another. This may also be done in a number of ways:

a. Have couples write out their specific prayer requests on the Prayer Request Forms (or index cards). These requests may then be shared with the whole group or traded with another couple as prayer partners for the week. If requests are shared with the whole group, pray as a group before adjourning the meeting; if requests are traded, allow time for the prayer-partner couples to pray together.

b. Gather the whole group together and lead couples in guided prayer.

c. Have individual couples pray together.

d. Split the members into two groups by gender. Have them pray over their marriages, asking God to reveal any points where they might be acting unfaithful toward their spouse.

After the Meeting

1. **Evaluate**—Spend time evaluating the meeting's effectiveness (found in *The Focus on the Family Marriage Ministry Guide*, "Reproducible Forms" section).

2. **Encourage**—During the week, try to contact each couple (through phone calls, notes of encouragement, e-mails or instant messaging) and welcome them to the group. Make yourself available to answer any questions or concerns they may have and generally get to know them. This contact might best be done by the husband-leader contacting the men and the wife-leader contacting the women.

3. **Equip**—Complete the Bible study, even if you have previously gone through this study together.

4. **Pray**—Prayerfully prepare for the next meeting, praying for each couple and your own preparation. Discuss with the Lord any apprehension, excitement or anything else that is on your mind regarding your Bible study material and/or the group members. If you feel inadequate or unprepared, ask for strength and insight. If you feel tired or burdened, ask for God's light yoke. Whatever it is you need, ask God for it. He will provide!

> **Reminder:** *In your desire to serve the members of your group, don't neglect your own marriage. Spend quality time with your spouse during the week!*

Session Two | The Mystery of Submission

Before the Meeting

1. Gather pens or pencils, paper, 3x5-inch index cards and Bibles.
2. Make photocopies of the Prayer Request Form or provide index cards for recording requests.
3. Read through your own answers from the session and mark the ones that you especially want to have the group discuss. Also highlight any key verses you feel are appropriate to share.
4. Prepare slips of paper with references for the verses that you will want someone to read aloud during the session. Distribute these slips as group members arrive, but be sensitive to those who are uncomfortable reading aloud or who might not be familiar with the Bible.

Ice Breakers

1. Hand a Prayer Request Form (or index card) to each member as he or she enters the room. Encourage them to at least fill in their name and phone number, even if they don't have any requests. Remind members that everyone needs someone to pray for them, even if there is no specific need.
2. Invite couples to share how they applied to their marriage relationship what they learned in last week's session.
3. Ask volunteers to share one praise or good thing that happened during the past week. This is a good chance for those who might not always see the good in things to learn how to express gratitude and thanksgiving to God, no matter what the circumstance.
4. Begin with prayer.

Discussion

1. **Tilling the Ground**—Invite volunteers to share their answers to questions 1 and 2. Invite others to share their answers to question 3.

2. **Planting the Seed**—Have group members form two smaller groups based on gender to discuss questions 4 through 21. Invite members to pair up with an accountability partner of the same gender to call during the week to encourage one another.

3. **Watering the Hope**—Bring the whole group back together to discuss questions 22 through 24.

4. **Harvesting the Fruit**—Invite group members to join with their spouse to share their affirmations with one another.

5. **Close in Prayer**—Distribute Prayer Request Forms (or index cards) and allow time for couples to pray together for the members whose prayer requests they have received.

After the Meeting

1. **Evaluate**—Spend time evaluating the meeting's effectiveness.

2. **Encourage**—During the week, try to contact each couple, encouraging them to contact their prayer partners.

3. **Equip**—Complete the Bible study.

4. **Pray**—Prayerfully prepare for the next meeting, praying for each couple and your own preparation.

Session Three | The Mission of Self-Sacrifice

Before the Meeting

1. Gather pens or pencils, paper, 3x5-inch index cards and Bibles.
2. Make photocopies of the Prayer Request Form or provide index cards for recording requests.
3. Read through your own answers from the session and mark the ones that you especially want to have the group discuss. Also highlight any key verses you feel are appropriate to share.
4. Prepare slips of paper with references for the verses that you will want someone to read aloud during the session. Distribute these slips as group members arrive, but be sensitive to those who are uncomfortable reading aloud or who might not be familiar with the Bible.
5. Obtain a newsprint pad or poster board and a felt-tip pen or use a white board or chalkboard.
6. Prepare a brief testimony of how you came to know Jesus as Savior and Lord of your life. Or call a member of the group and ask if he or she would share a brief testimony.

Ice Breakers

1. Hand a Prayer Request Form (or index card) to each member as he or she enters the room.
2. Share, or have the member you contacted share, the testimony of how you (or he or she) came to accept Jesus as Savior.

Discussion

1. **Tilling the Ground**—Encourage members to share their answers to questions 1 and 2. Invite one volunteer to share his or her answer to question 3.
2. **Planting the Seed**—Discuss questions 4 through 13 with the whole group.

3. **Watering the Garden**—Have each couple pair up with another couple to discuss questions 4 through 6. Have each foursome share their response to at least one of the incidents.
4. **Harvesting the Fruit**—Allow time for individual couples to share their answers with one another.
5. **Close in Prayer**—Have couples rejoin the couple with whom they shared the Watering the Garden discussion. Instruct them to swap Prayer Request Forms (or index cards) and spend a few minutes in prayer together. Encourage each couple to call their prayer-partner couple during the week and share any praises, results or further requests.

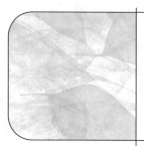

Note: Be sensitive to group members who might not know Christ as Savior and Lord. Be available after the meeting to answer any questions they might have concerning their relationship with God. Be open to the Holy Spirit's leading in asking if anyone would like to make a commitment or rededication to the Lord at this time.

After the Meeting

1. **Evaluate**.
2. **Encourage**—During the week, call each couple and ask if they have called their prayer partners. Encourage them as they continue to complete the study. If anyone accepted Christ during the meeting, follow up by making an appointment to meet with him or her. Caution: It is best that you and your spouse meet with individuals together. Or you could meet one-on-one with the person of the same gender.
3. **Equip**—Complete the Bible study.
4. **Pray**—Prayerfully prepare for the next meeting, praying for each couple and your own preparation. Whatever it is you need, ask God for it. He will provide!

Session Four | Christ Is Our Model

Before the Meeting

1. Gather pens or pencils, paper, 3x5-inch index cards and Bibles.
2. Make photocopies of the Prayer Request Form or provide index cards for recording requests.
3. Make photocopies of the Study Review Form (see *The Focus on the Family Marriage Ministry Guide*, "Reproducible Forms" section).
4. Read through your own answers from the session and mark the ones that you especially want to have the group discuss. Also highlight any key verses you feel are appropriate to share.
5. Prepare slips of paper with references for the verses that you will want someone to read aloud during the session. Distribute these slips as group members arrive, but be sensitive to those who are uncomfortable reading aloud or who might not be familiar with the Bible.

Ice Breakers

1. Hand a Prayer Request Form (or index card) to each member as he or she enters the room.
2. Invite members to share any praises or results for their prayer requests from the previous session.
3. Form two smaller groups and have them brainstorm the definitions of "joy" and "happiness." After about two minutes have them share their definitions with the whole group.

Discussion

1. **Tilling the Ground**—Discuss questions 1 through 3 with the whole group.
2. **Planting the Seed**—Have each couple pair up with another couple (if possible, with their prayer partners for the past week) and discuss questions 4 through 14.

3. **Watering the Hope**—Bring the whole group together to discuss the story of David and Vi. Have them brainstorm ideas about how they could help couples in similar situations.

4. **Harvesting the Fruit**—Invite individual couples to privately share their answers to questions 18 and 19.

5. **Close in Prayer**—Bring the whole group together. Invite sentence prayers of praise and thanksgiving. For the benediction, read aloud Ephesians 5:1-2: "Be imitators of God, therefore, as dearly loved children and live a life of love, just as Christ loved us and gave himself up for us as a fragrant offering and sacrifice to God."

After the Meeting

1. **Evaluate**—Distribute the Study Review Forms for members to take home with them. Share about the importance of feedback, and ask members to take the time this week to write their review of the group meetings and then to return them to you.

2. **Encourage**—Call each couple during the next week and invite them to join you for the next study in the *Focus on the Family Marriage Series*.

3. **Equip**—Begin preparing and brainstorming new activities for the next Bible study.

4. **Pray**—Praise the Lord for the work He has done in the lives of the couples in the study. Continue to pray for these couples as they apply the lessons learned in the last few weeks.

Note
1. Al Janssen, *The Marriage Masterpiece* (Wheaton, IL: Tyndale House Publishers, 2001).

Welcome to the Family!

As you participate in the *Focus on the Family Marriage Series*, it is our prayerful hope that God will deepen your understanding of His plan for marriage and that He will strengthen your marriage relationship.

This series is just one of the many helpful, insightful, and encouraging resources produced by Focus on the Family. In fact, that's what Focus on the Family is all about—providing inspiration, information, and biblically based advice to people in all stages of life.

It began in 1977 with the vision of one man, Dr. James Dobson, a licensed psychologist and author of 18 best-selling books on marriage, parenting, and family. Alarmed by the societal, political, and economic pressures that were threatening the existence of the American family, Dr. Dobson founded Focus on the Family with one employee and a once-a-week radio broadcast aired on only 36 stations.

Now an international organization, the ministry is dedicated to preserving Judeo-Christian values and strengthening and encouraging families through the life-changing message of Jesus Christ. Focus ministries reach families worldwide through 10 separate radio broadcasts, two television news features, 13 publications, 18 Web sites, and a steady series of books and award-winning films and videos for people of all ages and interests.

We'd love to hear from you!

For more information about the ministry, or if we can be of help to your family, simply write to Focus on the Family, Colorado Springs, CO 80995 or call 1-800-A-FAMILY (1-800-232-6459). Friends in Canada may write Focus on the Family, P.O. Box 9800, Stn. Terminal, Vancouver, B.C. V6B 4G3 or call 1-800-661-9800. Visit our Web site—www.family.org—to learn more about Focus on the Family or to find out if there is an associate office in your country.

Strengthen and enrich your marriage with these Focus on the Family® relationship builders.

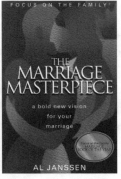

The Marriage Masterpiece

Now that you've discovered the richness to be had in "The Focus on the Family Marriage Series" Bible studies, be sure to read the book the series is based on. *The Marriage Masterpiece* takes a fresh appraisal of the exquisite design God has for a man and woman. Explaining the reasons why this union is meant to last a lifetime, it also shows how God's relationship with humanity is the model for marriage. Rediscover the beauty and worth of marriage in a new light with this thoughtful, creative book. A helpful study guide is included for group discussion. Hardcover.

The Love List

Marriage experts Drs. Les and Leslie Parrot present eight healthy habits that refresh, transform and restore the intimacy of your marriage relationship. Filled with practical suggestions, this book will help you make daily, weekly, monthly and yearly improvements in your marriage. Hardcover.

Capture His Heart/Capture Her Heart

Lysa TerKeurst has written two practical guides—one for wives and one for husbands—that will open your eyes to the needs, desires and longings of your spouse. These two books each offer eight essential criteria plus creative tips for winning and holding his or her heart. Paperback set.

• • •

STRENGTHEN MARRIAGES.
STRENGTHEN YOUR CHURCH.

Here's Everything You Need for a Dynamic Marriage Ministry!

Focus on the Family ® Marriage Series Group Starter Kit
Kit Box • Bible Study/Marriage • ISBN 08307.32365

Group Starter Kit includes:

• Seven Bible Studies: *The Masterpiece Marriage, The Passionate Marriage, The Fighting Marriage, The Model Marriage, The Surprising Marriage, The Giving Marriage* and *The Covenant Marriage*

• *The Focus on the Family Marriage Ministry Guide*

• *An Introduction to the Focus on the Family Marriage Series* video

Pick up the *Focus on the Family Marriage Series* where Christian books are sold.

Gospel Light

Devotionals for Drawing Near to God and One Another

Moments Together for Couples
Hardcover • 384p
ISBN 08307.17544

Moments Together for Parents
Gift Hardcover
96p
ISBN 08307.32497

Moments Together for Intimacy
Gift Hardcover
96p
ISBN 08307.32489

Give Your Marriage a Checkup

The Marriage Checkup
How Healthy
Is Your Marriage Really?
Paperback • 140p
ISBN 08307.30699

The Marriage Checkup Questionnaire
An Easy-to-Use Questionnaire
to Help You Evaluate the
Health of Your Marriage
Manual • 24p
ISBN 08307.30648

How to Counsel a Couple in 6 Sessions or Less
A Tool for Marriage Counseling
to Use in Tandem with the
Marriage Checkup Questionnaire
Manual • 24p
ISBN 08307.30680

Complete Your Marriage-Strengthening Library

Preparing for Marriage
The Complete Guide
to Help You Discover God's Plan
for a Lifetime of Love
Dennis Rainey
Paperback • 170p
ISBN 08307.17803
Counselor's Pack
(3 books, I Leader's Guide)
ISBN 08307.21568
Couples Pack (2 books) • ISBN 08307.21576
Leader's Guide • ISBN 08307.17609

Communication: Key to Your Marriage
A Practical Guide to Creating
a Happy, Fulfilling Relationship
Dr. H. Norman Wright
Paperback • 244p
ISBN 08307.25334
Video Approx. 2 hrs.
UPC 607135.004639

Holding on to Romance
Keeping Your Marriage
Alive and Passionate
After the Honeymoon Years
Dr. H. Norman Wright
Video • Approx. 1 hr.
UPC 85116.00779

 **Gospel Light**